SPOTTER'S GUIDE TO
BUTTERFLIES

George E. Hyde
Illustrated by Joyce Bee

Additional illustrations by Christine Howes
and Ian Jackson

Edited by Michelle Bates, Su Swallow and Sue Tarsky
Series editor: Philippa Wingate
Designed by Andrea Slane
Cover design and series designer: Laura Fearn
Cover illustrations by Ian Jackson
With thanks to Neil Francis

Picture acknowledgements, backgrounds - pages 2-3, 12-64 © Digital Vision;
page 1 © Corbis (William Dow); pages 6-7, 9 © Corbis (Dan Guravich).

First published in 2000 by Usborne Publishing Ltd., Usborne House,
83-85 Saffron Hill, London EC1N 8RT, England. www.usborne.com

Printed in Spain

CONTENTS

This beautiful African butterfly is a Citrus Swallowtail.

3

HOW TO USE THIS BOOK

This book is an identification guide to some of the butterflies of Britain and Europe. You can take it with you when you go spotting.

Peacock butterfly

The markings are like the "eyes" on a peacock's tail

The butterflies are arranged by family to make it easier for you to look them up. This Peacock butterfly, for example, is a member of the Admiral family and comes under the heading "Fritillaries and Admirals". Sometimes the caterpillar is also shown with the plant that it feeds from.

The pictures are drawn at life size (except where the text tells you otherwise).

Each butterfly is shown both with its wings open and with them closed, because the wing markings on the underside are often quite different from those on the upperside.

If male and female butterflies of the same kind vary, both are shown to help you to identify them. (The symbol ♂ means male and the symbol ♀ means female.)

HOW BUTTERFLIES ARE DESCRIBED

Each butterfly in this book
has a picture and a
description to help you to
identify it. The example
below shows you how the
descriptions work.

This is the wingspan
(W.S.) measured in mm

Name and description
of butterfly

Wings
closed

➡ BROWN ARGUS

Usually flies on chalk
downs and limestone
hills where rock grows.
Visits flowers on
warm sunny days.
Flies fast.
W.S. 28-30 mm.

Caterpillar

Average wingspan

Circle to tick when you
spot this butterfly

AREAS COVERED BY THIS BOOK

The green area on this
map shows the countries
which are covered by this
book. However, not all of
the butterflies that inhabit
these countries are
included, in which case
the description will tell you
that it is "not in Britain".

Scandinavia

British
Isles

Mainland
Europe

5

WHAT TO TAKE

When you go out to spot butterflies, take this book, a notepad and a pencil with you so that you can record your finds.

Look for butterflies in spring and summer. A good time to see them is in the evening, when many of them rest on grasses. Keep a detailed record of the butterflies you find and note down when and where you found them. Drawing the butterflies might help you to identify them later.

Make sure that you note down the different markings on the wings to help you determine whether they are male or female. If you see a butterfly that is not in this book, your notes will help you to identify it from other books later. Don't try to catch the butterflies. For tips about attracting butterflies, see pages 56-57.

Monarch butterflies

SCORECARD

The scorecard at the end of this book gives you a score for each butterfly you spot. A common butterfly scores 5 points, and a very rare one scores 25 points. If you like, you can add up your score after a day out spotting.

Species (Name of butterfly)	Score	Date spotted
Adonis Blue	20	5/7/00
Amanda's Blue	25	20/7/00
Apollo	25	26/7/00

Fill in the scorecard like this

LIFE CYCLE

Butterflies hatch from eggs. Before they become adult, they go through different stages of growth. Their life cycle consists of egg, larva and pupa stages before an adult butterfly emerges.

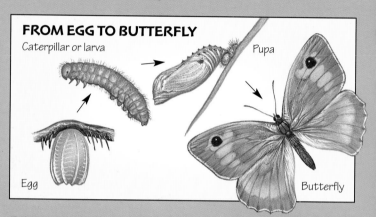

FROM EGG TO BUTTERFLY

Caterpillar or larva

Pupa

Egg

Butterfly

EGG

After mating, a female butterfly lays her eggs singly, or in clusters, on a plant.

When they hatch, the caterpillars feed on this plant. The eggs can hatch within any time from a few days to a couple of weeks.

Butterfly eggs

Usually the eggs are laid on the underside of the leaf where they are protected from bad weather and predators.

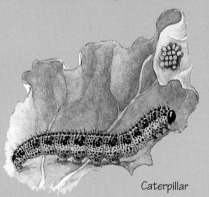

Caterpillar

➡ CATERPILLAR

A caterpillar spends most of its time feeding. It sheds its skin several times as it grows. When the caterpillar is fully grown, it stops feeding and changes into a pupa.

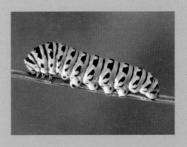

⬅ PUPA

A pupa does not move, eat or drink. This makes it particularly vulnerable to attacks from a variety of other animals. Inside the pupa, the caterpillar slowly turns into a butterfly.

A pupa is fixed to a plant stem or a fence by a sticky thread

➡ BUTTERFLY

An adult butterfly hatches out in spring or summer. The pupa skin splits and the damp butterfly crawls out. It rests for an hour or two while its wings expand and harden and then it is ready to fly off.

This Swallowtail butterfly has just hatched from its pupa

FEEDING

Caterpillars feed on the leaves of the plant on which they hatch. Some caterpillars spin a tent of silk on the leaf as they feed, and make the tent larger as they need more food.

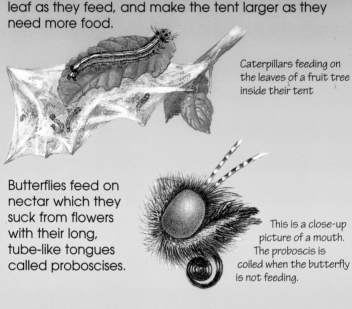

Caterpillars feeding on the leaves of a fruit tree inside their tent

Butterflies feed on nectar which they suck from flowers with their long, tube-like tongues called proboscises.

This is a close-up picture of a mouth. The proboscis is coiled when the butterfly is not feeding.

Small Tortoiseshell butterfly

Some species, like the Red Admirals and Peacocks, also enjoy eating rotting fruit. All butterflies need water, and you may see butterflies drinking from wet stones or from the bottoms of leaf stems.

PROTECTION

Caterpillars and butterflies use different methods to protect themselves. Some of them are camouflaged to look like twigs or leaves. This makes them hard to see.

This bird is pecking at a Hairstreak's false head

Hairstreak butterflies have a false head at the back of their wings to confuse birds

The Comma butterfly looks like a dead leaf when its wings are closed

Others have bright markings to frighten their enemies away. Many butterflies have spots like eyes on their wings to distract birds from their bodies. Some caterpillars are hairy, which birds find distasteful.

Owl butterfly

This Meadow Brown butterfly has been damaged by a bird's beak. The bird attacked the bright spot on the wing, not the body, so the insect escaped.

MONARCH

➡ **MONARCH**
Also called Milkweed.
Visitor from America and
the largest butterfly found
in Britain. Visits bramble,
ragwort and other
flowers. Open places.
Rare.
W.S. 103-106 mm.

Lesser
burdock

12

BROWNS

➡ WALL BROWN
Often rests on walls
and paths. Likes rough,
open ground and
woodland glades.
Flies slowly.
Caterpillar eats grasses.
W.S. 44-46 mm.

Caterpillar

**➡ LARGE WALL
BROWN**
Often settles on stony
paths in hills and
mountains.
Not in Britain.
W.S. 50-56 mm.

13

BROWNS

Thyme

♀

Mat grass

♀

♂

➤ MOUNTAIN RINGLET
Likes moorland flowers.
Often rests on grass with
wings open to sun itself.
In Lake District and
Scottish mountains.
W.S. 35-38mm.

♂

Caterpillar

♂

♂

Blue mountain grass

♀

➤ SCOTTISH ARGUS
Flies only in sunshine
and hides in grass on
dull days. Open
conifer woods in hilly
places. Caterpillar
eats grasses.
W.S. 45-50 mm.

♀

Caterpillar

14

Orange-brown
European form

♂

♀

➡ SPECKLED WOOD

Likes bramble flowers.
Often settles on sun-
spotted leaves in
woods and forests.
Caterpillar eats grasses.
W.S. 47-50 mm.

♂

♀

Bramble

➡ ARRAN BROWN

May visit flowers but rests
mostly on grasses. Open
grassland, near
woods or forests.
Rare visitor to Scotland.
W.S. 48-54 mm.

BROWNS

♀

♂

♀

♂

➡ GRAYLING
May visit field scabious
and other flowers, but
mostly rests on the ground
with wings closed.
Sandy places and
chalk downs.
W.S. 56-61 mm.

Lucerne

**➡ GREAT BANDED
GRAYLING**
Likes lucerne and other
flowers, but mostly rests
on the ground with
closed wings. Open
woodland.
Not in Britain.
W.S. 66-72 mm.

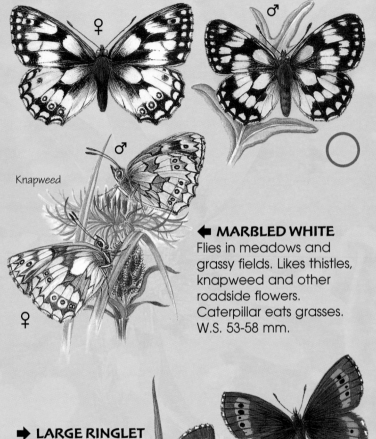

♀

♂

♂

Knapweed

♀

← MARBLED WHITE
Flies in meadows and
grassy fields. Likes thistles,
knapweed and other
roadside flowers.
Caterpillar eats grasses.
W.S. 53-58 mm.

➡ LARGE RINGLET
Rests mainly on
grasses.
In mountains.
Caterpillar eats
grasses.
Not in Britain.
W.S. 42-46 mm.

17

BROWNS

♂ ♀

♂ ♀

➡ MEADOW BROWN
Meadows and grassy
places where it visits
thistles, knapweed
and bramble flowers.
Active even on dull days.
Caterpillar eats grasses.
W.S. 50-55 mm.

Bramble

◀ RINGLET
Keeps to damp, grassy
places and sunny
woodland paths.
Visits thistles,
knapweed and
bramble flowers.
W.S. 48-52 mm.

Thistle

Hawkweed

◀ SMALL HEATH
Not fussy about where it
lives, and found in open
woods, on marshes
and on dry hillsides.
Likes hawkweed.
W.S. 33-35 mm.

**◀ GATEKEEPER
or HEDGE BROWN**
Basks in sunshine on
roadside hedges,
especially on bramble.
Most commmon in
the south.
W.S. 40-46 mm.

Bramble

Heather

The colours of this
butterfly vary a lot

◀ LARGE HEATH
Sometimes visits heath
flowers, but mostly rests
on grasses with wings
closed. Likes damp
places. Caterpillar eats
moorland grasses.
W.S. 33-35mm.

FRITILLARIES & ADMIRALS

◀ QUEEN OF SPAIN FRITILLARY
Rare visitor from Europe.
Likes clover and lucerne.
On rough grassland.
Caterpillar eats wild pansy.
W.S. 46-53 mm.

Red clover

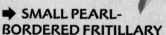
Spots look silver

➡ SMALL PEARL-BORDERED FRITILLARY
Visits summer flowers in damp grassy places, in and around woods. Caterpillar eats violet leaves.
W.S. 42-44 mm.

Violet

Ground ivy

◀ PEARL-BORDERED FRITILLARY
Visits spring flowers in dry woodland. Like Small Pearl-bordered, but has fewer pearly spots under its wings.
W.S. 42-46mm.

The butterflies on this page are smaller than life size

♀ ♀ ♂

➡ DARK GREEN FRITILLARY

Likes thistle and bramble
flowers. Open grassland
near woods, and high
rough ground.
Flies fast.
W.S. 63-70mm.

Thistle

♂

Bracken

♀

Dark
female form

Violet

➡ SILVER-WASHED FRITILLARY

Likes bramble flowers.
Rests on bracken with
open wings. Woods in
southern England.
Strong flier.
W.S. 72-76 mm.

♂ **♀**

Bramble

21

FRITILLARIES & ADMIRALS

◀ VIOLET FRITILLARY
Visits spring flowers in light woodland, on heaths and in meadows. Often in hilly places. Not in Britain.
W.S. 32-34 mm.

➡ NIOBE FRITILLARY
Likes thistles. In grassy places on mountains, but only up as high as trees grow.
Not in Britain.
W.S. 48-60 mm.

Violet

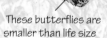

These butterflies are smaller than life size

Thistle

◀ CARDINAL FRITILLARY
Likes thistles and lime tree flowers. Look for it in flowery meadows. Caterpillar eats leaves of violets.
Not in Britain.
W.S. 72-80mm.

➡ HEATH FRITILLARY
Only found in woodland where the caterpillar's foodplant, cow-wheat, grows. Can be found in southern Britain, but very rare and endangered. Caterpillars are eaten by pheasants. W.S. 40-44 mm.

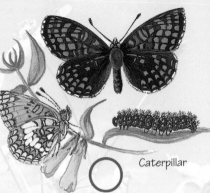

Caterpillar

Cow-wheat

Devil's bit scabious

⬅ MARSH FRITILLARY
Visits spring flowers in light marshy places. Lives in colonies (or groups). Notice shiny wings. Caterpillar eats devil's bit scabious and honeysuckle. W.S. 42-48 mm.

➡ GLANVILLE FRITILLARY
Rough grassy slopes by the sea. Only found on the south coast of the Isle of Wight. Caterpillar feeds on plantains. W.S. 41-45 mm.

Plantain

Caterpillar

23

FRITILLARIES & ADMIRALS

← HIGH BROWN FRITILLARY
Very fond of thistle flowers. In woods, where it may sleep on high branches on dull days. Caterpillar eats violet leaves. W.S. 60-68 mm.

♀

♂

Thistle

➡ PEACOCK
Common in gardens. One of five British species that hibernates in adult stage, in hollow trees, sheds, etc. Caterpillar eats nettles. W.S. 62-68 mm.

The markings are like the "eyes" on a peacock's tail

← PAINTED LADY
Arrives in spring from
North Africa. Lays eggs
on thistles. Adult
insects can be seen
in autumn, but
do not survive
the winter.
W.S. 62-65 mm.

Thistle

➡ RED ADMIRAL
Common in gardens
on buddleia and
Michaelmas daisies.
Migrates here from
the Mediterranean.
Caterpillar feeds
on nettles.
W.S. 66-68 mm.

Thistle

**← SMALL
TORTOISESHELL**
Name comes from pattern
on wings. Visits many
flowers and is common all
over Britain. On the wing
from April to November.
W.S. 48-52 mm.

25

FRITILLARIES & ADMIRALS

← LARGE TORTOISESHELL
Very rare. Likes bramble flowers. Rests on leaves of tall trees in lanes and edges of woods. Caterpillars feed on elm and goat willow. W.S. 62-66 mm.

The butterflies on this page are slightly smaller than life size

↑ CAMBERWELL BEAUTY
Rare visitor from Scandinavia, and does not breed in Britain. Yellow wing borders turn white with age. Riverbanks and orchards. W.S. 70-73 mm.

➡ CRANBERRY FRITILLARY

In bogs and swampy places. Lays eggs on cranberry, which the caterpillar feeds on. Not in Britain. W.S. 34-42 mm.

♀

Cranberry

♂

♂

Meadowsweet

♀

⬅ LESSER MARBLED FRITILLARY

In damp meadows and marshy places. Caterpillar feeds mainly on meadowsweet. Not in Britain. W.S. 34-40 mm.

FRITILLARIES & ADMIRALS

♀

← COMMA
Easy to recognize by its ragged wing edges and the shape of a letter "c" on underside of its wings. In woods and gardens. W.S. 56-58 mm.

♂

When Lesser Purple Emperor's wings catch the light they shimmer purple

Smaller than life-size

→ LESSER PURPLE EMPEROR
Does not visit flowers, but drinks from puddles and may settle on dead animals. In woods. Lays eggs on poplar and willow. Not in Britain. W.S. 66-70 mm.

Willow

These butterflies are smaller than life size

← PURPLE EMPEROR

One of Britain's largest butterflies. Drinks from woodland puddles. Males fly around tree tops. Caterpillar eats goat willow leaves. W.S. 76-84 mm.

Cowslip

→ DUKE OF BURGUNDY FRITILLARY

Visits cowslip and bugle in open woods. Male walks on four legs, female on all six. Caterpillar eats cowslip. W.S. 30-32 mm.

FRITILLARIES & ADMIRALS

Strawberry tree

The butterflies on this page are smaller than life size

➤ TWO-TAILED PASHA

Rare. Near Mediterranean and North African coasts. Male very active and flies fast. Caterpillar lives on strawberry tree. W.S. 76-82 mm.

BLUES

➡ SMALL BLUE
Britain's smallest butterfly.
Adult and caterpillar both
seen on kidney vetch.
Found in groups on
downs and rough grass.
W.S. 20-28 mm.

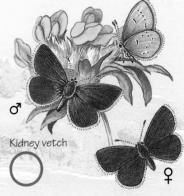

Kidney vetch

⬅ IDAS BLUE
Visits trefoil and other
flowers on mountain
slopes. Caterpillar eats
trefoil, and later lives in
ants' nests.
Not in Britain.
W.S. 28-32 mm.

Bird's foot
trefoil

Cranberry

➡ CRANBERRY BLUE
Butterfly and caterpillar
both feed on cranberry,
which grows on moorland
and mountain slopes.
Not in Britain.
W.S. 26-28 mm.

BLUES

➡ MAZARINE BLUE
Flowery meadows and grassy slopes near the sea. Caterpillar lives in flowers of the pea family. A rare migrant to Britain.
W.S. 35-36 mm.

Red clover

◀ AMANDA'S BLUE
Flowery places on lowland and hills not higher than 1,600 m. Hibernates as a small caterpillar on tufted vetch. Not in Britain.
W.S. 32-38 mm.

Tufted vetch

➡ BROWN ARGUS

Usually flies on chalk downs and limestone hills where rock rose grows. Visits flowers on warm sunny days. Flies fast.
W.S. 28-30 mm.

♂

♀

♂

Caterpillar

Common rock rose

♀

Hoary rock rose

The markings of this butterfly vary – sometimes it has no white spots

⬅ MOUNTAIN ARGUS or NORTHERN BROWN ARGUS

Easily recognized by the white dot on front wing. Sheltered moorland and grassy roadsides in Scotland and northern England. Caterpillar feeds on rock rose.
W.S. 28-30 mm.

BLUES

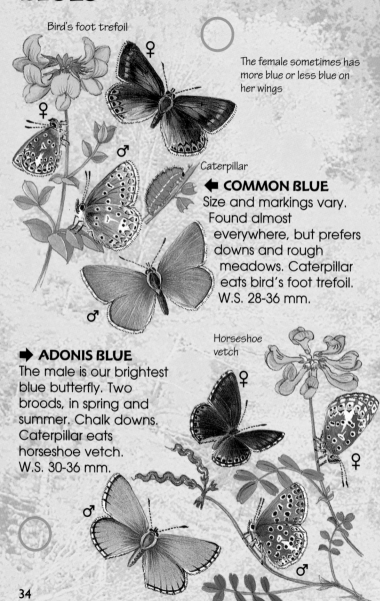

Bird's foot trefoil

♀

The female sometimes has more blue or less blue on her wings

♀

♂

Caterpillar

◀ COMMON BLUE
Size and markings vary. Found almost everywhere, but prefers downs and rough meadows. Caterpillar eats bird's foot trefoil. W.S. 28-36 mm.

♂

➡ ADONIS BLUE
The male is our brightest blue butterfly. Two broods, in spring and summer. Chalk downs. Caterpillar eats horseshoe vetch. W.S. 30-36 mm.

Horseshoe vetch

♀

♀

♂

♂

➡ CHALKHILL BLUE

On flowery chalk downs in August. Very varied markings. Caterpillar eats horseshoe vetch.
W.S. 36-40 mm.

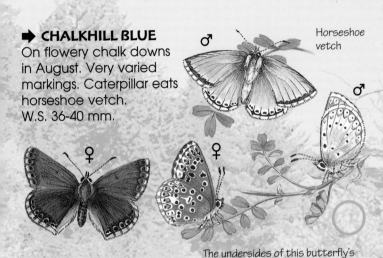

Horseshoe vetch

♂

♀

♂

♀

The undersides of this butterfly's wings vary in colour

Sweet pea

♂

⬅ IOLAS BLUE

Visits flowers of the pea family. In rocky hills and open woodland. Not in Britain.
W.S. 37-43 mm.

♀

BLUES

➡ SILVER-STUDDED BLUE

Likes to visit heather on open moors and sandy heaths. Caterpillar feeds on gorse flowers and other plants.
W.S. 29-31 mm.

The undersides of this butterfly's wings vary in colour

Heather

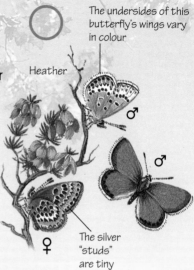

♂

Gorse

♀

♂

♀

The silver "studs" are tiny

♀

♀

Butterfly from second brood

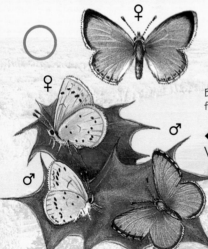

♀

♂

♂

⬅ HOLLY BLUE

Visits holly and ivy flowers and may drink by edges of streams. Gardens. Caterpillar feeds on unripe berries of holly and ivy.
W.S. 33-35 mm.

36

◀ LARGE BLUE
Very fond of wild thyme
flowers. Strong flyer.
Caterpillar feeds on
thyme and ant larvae.
Has been re-introduced
to Britain.
W.S. 38-46 mm.

♂

♀

The markings
can vary

♀

♀

♂

Thyme

➡ SCARCE COPPER
In meadows. Likes
goldenrod flowers.
Caterpillar feeds
on dock plants.
Not in Britain.
W.S. 32-34 mm.

♀

♂

♀

Dock

37

COPPERS

← PURPLE-EDGED COPPER

Lives in marshy places on lowland and hills up to 1,600 m. Caterpillar feeds on dock and bistort. Not in Britain. W.S. 32-38 mm.

♀

♀

♂

♂

Bistort

➡ SMALL COPPER

Easy to find all over Britain, especially on fleabane flowers. Female often larger than male. Caterpillar eats sorrel and dock. W.S. 26-30 mm.

♂

♀

Caterpillar

♂

♀

Sorrel

HAIRSTREAKS

➡ GREEN HAIRSTREAK

Hard to spot because of green underwings which camouflage it on leaves. Quite common on downs, moors, edges of woods, where gorse and broom grow. W.S. 31-34 mm.

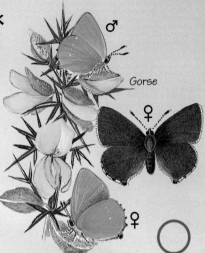

♂

Gorse

♀

♂

♀

⬅ BROWN HAIRSTREAK

Shy butterfly, not often seen flying. Rests on leaves of blackthorn in August and September. Edges of woods and hedges. W.S. 40-42 mm.

♀

♂

♂

Blackthorn

Notice the tails

♀

39

HAIRSTREAKS

♀

♂

Oak

♂

♀

← PURPLE HAIRSTREAK

Flies round tree tops in big oak woods. Rests on oak leaves and visits bramble flowers. Caterpillar eats oak leaves.
W.S. 36-39 mm.

→ BLACK HAIRSTREAK

Visits flowers of common privet and dogwood, but only found in a few places in the Midlands. Caterpillar eats blackthorn.
W.S. 36-37 mm.

♀

♂

Blackthorn

♂

♀

➡ WHITE LETTER HAIRSTREAK

Named after white mark, like a letter "w", on underside of hind wings. Often rests on leaves of wych elm. Open woods and lanes.
W.S. 34-35 mm.

♀

Notice the "W"

♂

Wych elm

♀

♂

♀

♂

⬅ BLUE-SPOT HAIRSTREAK

Likes rough, hilly places with bushes. Visits privet and other flowers. Caterpillar eats blackthorn. Not in Britian.
W.S. 29-33 mm.

♂

♀

41

SWALLOWTAILS

The butterflies on this page are smaller than life-size

← SWALLOWTAIL
Largest British butterfly, only found in Norfolk Broads. Caterpillar black when young, brightly coloured later.
Eats milk parsley.
W.S. 77-90 mm.

➡ SOUTHERN SWALLOWTAIL
Found on mountain sides. Rare, and only found in a few places in Europe.
Not in Britian.
W.S. 65-69 mm.

Hedge parsley

➡ SCARCE SWALLOWTAIL

On low and high ground, often near orchards. Visits blossoms of fruit trees. Caterpillar eats plum and blackthorn. Not in Britain. W.S. 70-84 mm.

Plum

Birthwort

⬅ SOUTHERN FESTOON

Rough, stony places. Caterpillar feeds on birthwort plants. Not in Britain. W.S. 50-52 mm.

This butterfly is smaller than life-size

SWALLOWTAILS

← APOLLO
Lives in mountains. Visits alpine plants, especially stone crop flowers. Not in Britain. W.S. 79-84 mm.

Orpine

➡ SMALL APOLLO
High up in mountains, often near streams or damp grassland. Visits alpine flowers. Not in Britain. W.S. 62-66 mm.

Reflexed stonecrop

WHITES & YELLOWS

The butterflies on this page are smaller than life-size

← BLACK-VEINED WHITE
No longer found in Britain, and declining in the rest of Europe. Caterpillar feeds on fruit trees and is often a pest in orchards.
W.S. 62-66 mm.

♂ Red clover

♀

♂

♀

Cabbage

♀

➡ LARGE WHITE
Visits garden flowers, but also flies in woods and open country. Caterpillar eats cabbage plants. Pupae often found on garden walls.
W.S. 62-64 mm.

♂

♀

WHITES & YELLOWS

➡ SMALL WHITE ♂
Appears in May and
August. Lays single
eggs on cabbages
and nasturtiums.
Common in gardens.
W.S. 48-50 mm.

♀

♀

♂

The butterflies on
this page are slightly
smaller than life-size

**⬅ GREEN-VEINED
WHITE**
Pattern on underwing
helps to protect the
butterfly from enemies
when it sits on grass.
Caterpillar eats leaves
and seed pods of
jack-by-the-hedge.
W.S. 47-50 mm.

♂

♀

♂

Wild mignonette

♀

♀

♂

♂

➡ BATH WHITE
Sometimes visits southern Britain, but rarely in large numbers. Fond of clover and wild mignonette flowers. W.S. 48-52 mm.

♂

○

♂

♀

➡ PEAK WHITE
Only found on grassy slopes high up in mountains. Visits wild mignonette. Not in Britain. W.S. 44-52 mm.

♀

○

WHITES & YELLOWS

← ORANGE TIP
Common in spring, often near cow parsley along hedgerows and edges of woods. Caterpillar eats seed pods of lady's smock. W.S. 42-48 mm.

♀

♂

♀

♂

Lady's smock

Yellow vetchling

♂

♀

➡ WOOD WHITE
Lives in woods, often in shady parts. Likes yellow vetchling and other woodland flowers. Weak flight. W.S. 40-42 mm.

♀

➡ PALE CLOUDED YELLOW

Rare visitor to Britain from southern Europe. Likes clover. Caterpillar cannot survive through our damp winter. W.S. 52-54 mm.

♀

Zigzag clover

♂

♂

The butterflies on this page are slightly smaller than life-size

♂

♀

Red clover

♂

♀

➡ CLOUDED YELLOW

Arrives here in spring from Mediterranean. Eggs laid on clover and lucerne. Second brood in autumn, but butterflies do not survive our winter. W.S. 58-62 mm.

The female's colour varies

WHITES & YELLOWS

♀

♂

♀

Horseshoe vetch

The butterflies on this page are slightly smaller than life-size

◀ BERGER'S CLOUDED YELLOW

Very like Pale Clouded Yellow, but even rarer. Chalk downs and limestone hills. Caterpillar eats horseshoe vetch. W.S. 52-54 mm.

♂

♀

♂

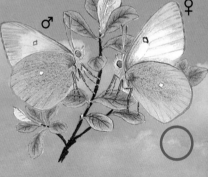

Whortleberry

♀

♂

➡ MOORLAND CLOUDED YELLOW

Lowland bogs and moors. Caterpillar feeds on bog whortleberry. Not in Britain. W.S. 53-55 mm.

The butterflies on this page are slightly smaller than life-size

Buckthorn

♀

♂

♀

➡ BRIMSTONE
Strong flight. Hedges and woodland paths. Hibernates as a butterfly in leafy bushes. Caterpillar feeds on buckthorn.
W.S. 58-60 mm.

♂

♂

♂

♀

Primrose

⬅ CLEOPATRA
Like the Brimstone, lives from June to the following spring. Mountains with open woods. Caterpillar eats buckthorn.
Not in Britain.
W.S. 58-60 mm.

♀

SKIPPERS

Wild strawberry

♀

♂

← GRIZZLED SKIPPER
Like all Skippers, it has skipping flight. Flowery, grassy places. Caterpillars eat wild strawberry.
W.S. 27-28 mm.

Jerusalem sage

♂

→ LARGE GRIZZLED SKIPPER
Visits flowers in waste ground. Flies from April to May. Caterpillar eats rock rose and cinquefoil.
Not in Britain.
W.S. 29-31 mm.

♀

Bird's foot trefoil

← DINGY SKIPPER
Looks more like a dull moth. Darts about rapidly among bugle and ground ivy flowers. Found on open ground and woodland paths.
W.S. 28-29 mm.

➡ CHEQUERED SKIPPER

Brighter than other Skippers. Likes bugle and suns itself on grasses in woods. Caterpillar eats brome grass.
Rare and protected.
W.S. 27-29 mm.

Bugle

♀

♂

Bugle

⬅ NORTHEREN CHEQUERED SKIPPER

Visits bugle and other spring flowers in woods and grassland. Caterpillar eats grasses.
Not in Britain.
W.S. 27-29 mm.

Wood false-brome

➡ LARGE CHEQUERED SKIPPER

Likes damp meadows full of flowers, and shady paths in woods. Often rests on grasses.
Not in Britain, except the Channel Islands.
W.S. 32-36 mm.

♂

♀

53

SKIPPERS

♀

♂

← ESSEX SKIPPER
Very like Small Skipper,
but antennae tips are
black underneath, not
brown. Visits thistles on
rough ground.
W.S. 26-27 mm.

Creeping
thistle

➡ SMALL SKIPPER
More common than Essex
Skipper. Visits flowers in
grassy fields inland and
near the sea.
Caterpillar eats
grasses.
W.S. 28-29 mm.

Grasses

♀

♂

← LULWORTH SKIPPER
First found near Lulworth
Cove in Dorset. Only flies
near coasts of Dorset and
Devon. Rests with wings
nearly open, or open.
W.S. 23-26 mm.

➡ LARGE SKIPPER

Commonest Skipper. Visits bramble and thistle flowers in grassy lanes and open woodland. Flies from June to August. W.S. 30-32 mm.

Stalkless thistle

⬅ SILVER-SPOTTED SKIPPER

Looks like Large Skipper, but has silver spots on underside of hind wings. Has become rare in Britain. Often rests on grasses. W.S. 31-33 mm.

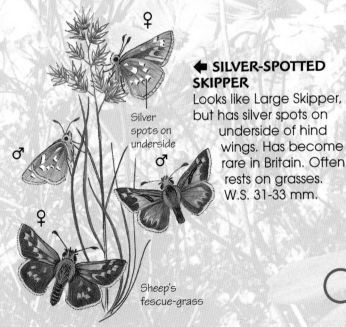

Silver spots on underside

Sheep's fescue-grass

ATTRACTING BUTTERFLIES

Some flowers, such as the ones shown here, are especially attractive to butterflies because they have bright colours and a strong scent.

You could encourage butterflies to visit your garden by planting some of these flowers. Make a record of which butterflies you see each month, how many of each species there are, and which flowers they visit.

You will soon notice which are the favourite flowers of each kind of butterfly. A few flowers, like buddleia, phlox and Michaelmas daisies, attract lots of species.

You could also leave a corner of your garden free to grow wild with uncut grass to encourage butterflies to lay their eggs there.

Small White

Brimstone
on aubretia

Small
Tortoishell
on buddleia

A patch of stinging nettles might encourage particular butterflies like the Small Tortoiseshell, the Peacock and the Red Admiral.

Do not use poison sprays on your flowers because these can kill butterflies.

Small Copper on Michaelmas daisy

Green-veined White on wallflower

Ice Plant

Red Admiral

Peacock

BUTTERFLY OR MOTH?

You can tell the difference between butterflies and moths by looking at their feelers, called antennae.

The antennae of butterlies always have knobs at the end. Moths' antennae are usually feathery or hair-like.

Butterflies also rest with their wings pressed tightly together over their bodies whereas most moths rest with their wings held tent-like over their bodies, or else with each wing spread out on either side. Also, most moths are not so brightly patterned as butterflies.

Moths usually have feathery antennae

Moth at rest with wings held tent-like over body

Butterflies usually have antennae with knobs

Butterfly with wings closed up over body

USEFUL WORDS

antenna (plural: antennae) – all butterflies have two antennae on the front of the head which they use for feeling and smelling.

camouflage – when the colours and shape of a butterfly, caterpillar or pupa match its background and make it difficult to see.

colony – a number of butterflies or caterpillars of the same kind living together.

hibernate – when a butterfly, caterpillar or pupa passes the winter in a sleep–like state.

larva (plural: larvae) – the larva, or caterpillar, hatches from the butterfly's egg, and the larval stage begins.

migrant – a butterfly that flies from one country to another, such as the Monarch, which flies from North America to visit Britain.

migration – the journey of certain butterflies from one country to another. Some butterflies migrate long distances.

moult – when a caterpillar sheds its skin as it grows larger.

nectar – a sweet liquid found in most flowers. Butterflies drink it.

proboscis – a butterfly's long, tube-like tongue, used for sucking nectar.

pupa (plural: pupae) – the fully-grown larva changes into a pupa, or chrysalis, and the pupa stage begins. The butterfly develops inside the pupa.

visitor – see **migrant**.

CLUBS AND WEB SITES

If you have access to the Internet, you can visit these Web sites to find out more about butterflies. For links to these sites, go to the Usborne Quicklinks Web site at **www.usborne-quicklinks.com** and enter the keywords "spotters butterflies".

Internet safety

When using the Internet, please follow the **Internet safety guidelines** shown on the Usborne Quicklinks Web site.

WEB SITE 1 The British Entomological and Natural History Society.

WEB SITE 2 The Amateur Entomologists Society's Bug Club for young enthusiasts.

WEB SITE 3 Learn about the spectacular migration of Monarch butterflies.

WEB SITE 4 Young and informative site about butterflies.

WEB SITE 5 A very informative site with fascinating information and interesting pictures.

WEB SITE 6 Information about the butterfly life cycle, and tropical butterflies, at the London Butterfly House.

WEB SITE 7 View an extensive butterfly collection and find out about butterfly habitats.

WEB SITE 8 A world atlas of butterflies, and lots of other useful information.

WEB SITE 9 The butterfly conservatory at the American Museum of Natural History.

SCORECARD

The butterflies on this scorecard are arranged in alphabetical order. Fill in the date on which you spot one beside its name. A common butterfly scores 5 points, and a rare one is worth 25. After a day's spotting, add up the points you have scored on a sheet of paper and keep a record of them. See if you can you score more points another day.

Species (Name of butterfly)	Score	Date spotted	Species (Name of butterfly)	Score	Date spotted
Adonis Blue	20		Clouded Yellow	20	
Amanda's Blue	25		Comma	15	
Apollo	25		Common Blue	5	
Arran Brown	20		Cranberry Blue	25	
Bath White	25		Cranberry Fritillary	25	
Berger's Clouded Yell.	25		Dark Green Fritillary	10	
Black Hairstreak	25		Dingy Skipper	10	
Black-veined White	25		Duke of Burgundy Frit.	15	
Blue-spot Hairstreak	25		Essex Skipper	20	
Brimstone	10		Gatekeeper	10	
Brown Argus	15		Glanville Fritillary	25	
Brown Hairstreak	20		Grayling	15	
Camberwell Beauty	25		Great Banded Grayling	25	
Cardinal Fritillary	25		Green Hairstreak	10	
Chalkhill Blue	15		Green-veined White	5	
Chequered Skipper	25		Grizzled Skipper	15	
Cleopatra	25		Heath Fritillary	25	

Species (Name of butterfly)	Score	Date spotted	Species (Name of butterfly)	Score	Date spotted
High Brown Fritillary	15		Orange Tip	10	
Holly Blue	10		Painted Lady	15	
Idas Blue	25		Pale Clouded Yellow	25	
Iolas Blue	25		Peacock	5	
Large Chequered Skip.	25		Peak White	25	
Large Grizzled Skipper	25		Pearl-bordered Fritillary	15	
Large Heath	20		Purple Emperor	25	
Large Ringlet	25		Purple Hairstreak	15	
Large Skipper	10		Purple-edged Copper	25	
Large Tortoiseshell	25		Queen of Spain Frit.	25	
Large Wall Brown	25		Red Admiral	10	
Large White	5		Ringlet	10	
Lesser Marbled Frit.	25		Scarce Copper	25	
Lesser Purple Emperor	25		Scarce Swallowtail	25	
Lulworth Skipper	20		Scottish Argus	20	
Marbled White	15		Silver-spotted Skipper	20	
Marsh Fritillary	20		Silver-studded Blue	15	
Mazarine Blue	25		Silver-washed Fritillary	15	
Meadow Brown	5		Small Apollo	25	
Monarch	25		Small Blue	15	
Moorland Clouded Yell.	25		Small Copper	10	
Mountain Argus	25		Small Heath	5	
Mountain Ringlet	20		Small Pearl bordered Frit.	15	
Niobe Fritillary	25		Small Skipper	10	
Northern Chequered Skip.	25		Small Tortoiseshell	5	